Helen

Why Do Monkeys Chatter?
and other questions about animals

WHY IS IT SO? Science

CAMBRIDGE UNIVERSITY PRESS

Contents

Questions about birds 4

Questions about reptiles 6

Questions about mammals 8

Questions about primates 10

It's a fact 12

Can you believe it? 14

Who found out? 16

It's quiz time! 20

Glossary 24

Questions about birds

a bald eagle flying

a black kite flying

Q: Why do birds have feathers?

A: Feathers help birds to fly. Wing feathers are a light but solid surface that can push against the air. When birds flap their wings down, the feathers close together, but when they flap up, the feathers separate to let air through.

Most birds have short tail and wing bones, but their feathers may be very long.

An eagle has long, wide wing feathers that help it to fly high in the air. It uses its tail feathers to help it to slow down or change direction.

Q: can all birds fly?

A: There are some birds that cannot fly. They **evolved** like this because their **habitat** did not have many **predators**. New Zealand has more birds that cannot fly than any other country. They include the kiwi, the kakapo, the takahe and several species of penguins.

Penguins are adapted for swimming and diving, so they can defend themselves. Ostriches, emus, cassowaries and rheas are large birds that cannot fly but they can run fast. Ostriches can also attack with their claws.

a kiwi

a penguin

an emu

Questions about reptiles

Q: What is the difference between an alligator and a crocodile?

A: Alligators and crocodiles both belong to the same species, crocodilians, but there are three differences between them. Alligators have wide, round, U-shaped snouts, but crocodiles have longer, more pointed, V-shaped snouts.

When its mouth is closed, you can't see the teeth in an alligator's lower jaw, but you can see them in a crocodile's.

Alligators prefer freshwater, but crocodiles usually live in saltwater habitats.

The alligator with its wide, rounded snout is at the top. The crocodile with its pointed snout is at the bottom.

an inland taipan

Q: Which is the most venomous snake?

A: Many people think the most **venomous** snake in the world is the inland taipan, which lives in Australia. Its bite has enough venom to kill 200,000 mice. In fact, the beaked sea snake has a more toxic venom, but its habitat (near many South Pacific Islands) is very remote, so people are not often bitten by it.

a beaked sea snake

How a python swallows an animal

A python first bites its prey and then holds it with its teeth. It coils around the animal and squeezes it to death. A python's jaw is very loose and its skin stretches so it can easily swallow an animal.

Questions about mammals

a platypus

an echidna

Q: Can mammals lay eggs?

A: Mammals do not usually lay eggs, but the platypus and echidna are mammals called monotremes which can lay eggs. They are very rare and only live in Australia and New Guinea.

The platypus spends a lot of time in water and it has webbed feet and a bill like a duck, waterproof fur and a flat tail.

Echidnas look like both porcupines and anteaters. They can have long or short beaks that they use to eat ants and termites.

The platypus and echidna are still mammals because they have lungs, are warm-blooded and **suckle** their young after they hatch from the eggs.

Q: Is a dolphin a mammal?

A: Yes – it spends all its time in water, but a dolphin is still a mammal and so are whales and porpoises. They are called cetaceans and all have lungs and breathe air through blowholes at the top of their heads.

Cetaceans can dive deep down in the water with one breath. They come up to breathe out and to take a long breath in before they dive down again.

Questions about primates

Q: Why do monkeys chatter?

A: Monkeys chatter to communicate with other monkeys about food or danger. They share ideas using cries and squawks.

Scientists have discovered that rhesus macaque monkeys on an island near Puerto Rico chatter to their relatives in a different way than to other monkeys. They listen carefully to their relatives and can identify them from the sounds they make. They also decide when to tell them where the best food is and when to help them if they are in danger.

a rhesus macaque monkey

a ring-tailed lemur

Q: Where do lemurs come from?

A: Nearly all lemurs live on Madagascar, an island off the east coast of Africa, and the nearby Comoros Islands. There are different habitats there, so some lemurs live in tropical rainforests and others live in places that are like deserts. There are many kinds of lemurs, but most of them have long, pointed noses, so they have a very good sense of smell.

a pygmy mouse lemur

an indri lemur

It's a fact

> Amazing marsupials
Kangaroos, brush-tailed possums and koalas are all **marsupials**. They have a **pouch** where their babies suckle. Most marsupials live in Australia.

> Polar bear capital
The town of Churchill in Manitoba, Canada is called the 'polar bear capital of the world' because people can see the bears going back to their natural habitat on the ice in autumn.

> Running on water
The basilisk is an iguana from Central America that escapes from predators by going where the predators cannot follow. It can run on water for several metres before it dives in and swims away.

> A huge diet

During the dry season an elephant eats between 150 and 170 kg of grass and woody plants each day. They also drink about 70 litres of water during that time. During the wet season they eat between 200 and 280 kg of food every day.

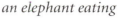
an elephant eating

a sloth bear

> Sloth bears

The sloth bear lives in India and Sri Lanka. It is the largest mammal that eats mainly termites. It uses its large lips and the gap between its front teeth to suck the termites out of their nests.

Lemmings

Lemmings produce four times more females than males. They only live for about two years, so they need more females to continue the species.

Can you believe it?

Monkey talk

There is a bird in Africa that can understand monkey chatter. The yellow-casqued hornbill is the first bird scientists know of that can understand the calls of another species well enough to recognise two different kinds of sound.

Still dangerous

The solenodon is a mammal that lives in Cuba and Hispanola. It looks like a big hedgehog, but has a venomous bite like a rattlesnake. Scientists thought they were extinct until 2003 when they found some were still alive.

a yellow-casqued hornbill

Look out!

Giraffes don't look very dangerous, but their long legs are very strong and can kill a lion.

Audiobat

There is a type of bat that can find the insects they want to eat from more than five metres away. They collect information about them by using **echolocation**. This is an audio sense that more than 800 varieties of bats can also use.

Looking after baby

Emperor penguins are the only animals that **breed** in Antarctica in the winter. The female lays her egg, and then the male stands close to the other males to keep the egg warm until it hatches. The females go into the sea to find food to bring back for the males and babies.

The male emperor penguin holds the egg on his feet to protect it from the winter cold. When it hatches, the baby stays in the male's brood pouch until it is bigger and can keep warm by itself.

Classifying animals website for kids:

http://www.hhmi.org/coolscience/forkids/critters/index.html

Who found out?

Orang-utans: Biruté Galdikas

Biruté Galdikas (1946–) was born in Germany, but grew up in Canada. She has studied orang-utans for over 34 years and has found that they like to be alone. An adult male's **range** is about 40 square kilometres and he can spend weeks going from tree to tree, eating fruit, leaves and insects, and never meet another orang-utan. The forests of Borneo, their habitat, have not changed, so they have always had food and space to continue to live alone.

Parrot expert: Irene Pepperberg

Irene Maxine Pepperberg (1949–) is an American scientist and wildlife **conservationist** who studies animals, especially parrots. She worked with an African Grey Parrot, Alex, and found that he could learn to speak like a two-year old child. Alex knew 150 words, could count up to seven, and could answer some questions. Dr Pepperberg says this shows that humans are not the only animals who can communicate ideas.

Marine biologist: Dr Isobel Bennett

Dr Isobel Bennett (1909–2008) was one of Australia's most famous **marine biologists**. She was one of the first women to go south with the Australian Antarctic Research expeditions. She first went to Macquarie Island in 1939 and returned three more times in the 1960s. Bennett carried out surveys at Jervis Bay and Ulladulla in New South Wales from 1974 to 1979. She also researched the Great Barrier Reef. Most of the things we know now about the reef and the animals that live there are because of her work.

Great Barrier Reef

Ethology: Konrad Lorenz

Konrad Lorenz (1903–1989) was one of the first people in the world to study **ethology**, looking at how animals behave in their natural habitats. In particular, he studied the way grey geese **bonded** to a parent figure, which he called imprinting. He saw that newborn chicks followed the first moving object they saw, and realised that this behaviour probably evolved to help young birds stay close to their parents where they were safer. Lorenz won a Nobel Prize for his work in 1973.

It's quiz time!

1 What is it? You can find all these animals in the Factbook.

1. It's the most venomous snake in the world. _____

2. It has webbed feet, a bill (like a duck), waterproof fur and a flat tail. _____

3. Nearly all of them live in Madagascar. They have long, pointed noses and a good sense of smell. _____

4. They are the only animals that breed in Antarctica in the winter. _____

5. They usually live in saltwater habitats. They have V-shaped snouts and when their mouths are shut you can see their teeth. _____

6. They like to be alone. _____

2 Write the animals in their groups.

~~alligator~~   crocodile   dolphin   eagle   echidna
emu   monkey   penguin   python

Reptiles	Birds	Mammals
alligator		

Which one of these animals is also a primate?

_____

3 True (T) or false (F)? Correct the false one(s).

1. Dolphins are fish. ___
   _____

2. Whales, dolphins and porpoises are mammals. ___
   _____

3. Whales, dolphins and porpoises take a long breath in before they dive deep down in the water. ___
   _____

4 Match the beginnings and endings of the sentences.

1. Birds that cannot fly evolved like that
2. A python can easily swallow an animal
3. A lemur has a good sense of smell
4. A giraffe can kill a lion

a) because it has a long, pointed nose.
b) because their habitat did not have many predators.
c) because its jaw is very loose and its skin stretches.
d) because its legs are very strong.

5 Write three sentences about your favourite animal.

_____
_____
_____
_____
_____
_____

Glossary

bonded: physically or emotionally attached to

breed: to have babies

conservationist: someone who protects animals and plants

echolocation: the location of objects by reflected sound, in particular used by animals such as dolphins and bats

ethology: the study of the behaviour of animals in their natural habitats

evolve: to develop over a very long time

habitat: natural home

marine biologist: someone who studies plants and animals in the ocean

marsupial: a mammal that has a pouch to hold and feed young

pouch: a pocket of skin

predator: an animal that eats other animals

range: the area in which an animal can live and move

suckle: to feed their young with mother's milk

venomous: able to bite or sting with poisonous fluid